Delta Force

BY LINDA BOZZO

amicus
high interest

Amicus High Interest is an imprint of Amicus
P.O. Box 1329, Mankato, MN 56002
www.amicuspublishing.us

Library of Congress Cataloging-in-Publication Data
Bozzo, Linda.
Delta Force / by Linda Bozzo.
     pages cm. – (Serving in the military)
Includes bibliographical references and index.
Summary: "An introduction to the life of Delta Force operators
in the US Army Special Operations Command (USASOC)
describing some missions, how they train, and their role in the
armed forces"– Provided by publisher.
ISBN 978-1-60753-491-4 (library bound) –
ISBN 978-1-60753-634-5 (ebook)
1. United States. Army. Delta Force–Juvenile literature. I. Title.
UA34.S64B6578 2015
356'.1670973–dc23

                          2013039229

Editor: Wendy Dieker
Series Designer: Kathleen Petelinsek
Book Designer: Steve Christensen
Photo Researcher: Kurtis Kinneman

Photo Credits: US Marines Photo/Alamy, Cover; Trinity Mirror/
Mirrorpix/Alamy, 5; Ed Darack/Science Faction/SuperStock,
6; Rafiq Maqbool/AP/Corbis, 8/9; US Marines Photo/
Alamy, 11; DoD/Corbis, 12; José Nicolas/Sygma/Corbis,
15; Stocktrek Images/Stocktrek Images/Corbis, 16/17; Ricki
Rosen/CORBIS SABA, 19; Yannick Tylle/Corbis, 20; Kevin
Lamarque/Reuters/Corbis, 23; Creator: Staff Sgt. Stacy L.
Pearsall, 24/25; DOD Photo/Alamy, 26; US Army Photo/
Alamy, 29

Printed in the United States at Corporate Graphics in North
Mankato, Minnesota.

10 9 8 7 6 5 4 3 2 1

Table of Contents

Kidnapped!

It was November 2004. American Roy Hallums was working in Iraq. **Terrorists** stormed into his building. They kidnapped him and five other men. Soon, the five men were set free. Now Roy is left. He is a **hostage**. The kidnappers want $12 million. Then they will let him go. Who can save Roy? The U.S. Army Delta Force can.

Roy Hallums was taken
from Baghdad, Iraq.

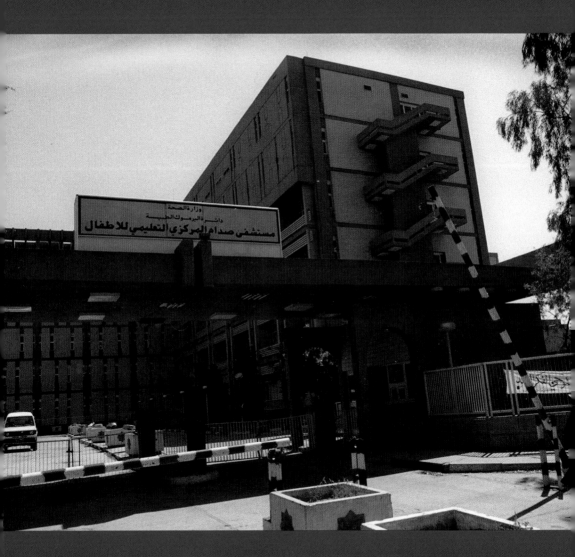

The chopper flies high
for a better view.

 How did Delta Force find Roy?

Roy is being held in a farmhouse. On September 7, 2005, the mission begins. Delta Force **operators** load a helicopter. They fly in. The chopper swoops down. The operators jump out. They bust into the farmhouse. The kidnappers are gone, nowhere to be found!

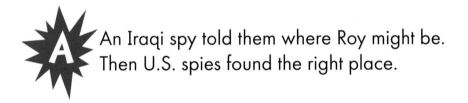
An Iraqi spy told them where Roy might be. Then U.S. spies found the right place.

But Delta Force finds
their man. Roy is in a tiny
room under the floor. A
slab of cement covers the
only door to the room.
Roy can't get out. A
skinny pipe sticks up from
the ground. It lets in his
only air. Operators break
through the cement.
They find Roy. Rescue
mission accomplished!

**A Delta Force team
searches the house.**

Elite Training

Delta Force is a small **unit** in the U.S. Army. Delta Force has two main jobs. One is to stop terrorists. The other is to rescue hostages.

Only the best soldiers are asked to join Delta. Some are Army Rangers. Others are Green Berets. Some are from special forces in the navy or air force. These men have already learned special skills. Delta training makes them even better.

These soldiers train for assault climbing.

Soldiers learn to fast-rope out of choppers. They can move quickly.

 Q Where do the members of Delta Force train?

Delta Force teams spend two years in hard training. They work on skills they already have. They practice rescue skills. They practice parachuting. They practice **fast-roping** out of a chopper. Delta teams learn to fight their way into buildings. They learn how to get out if things go wrong.

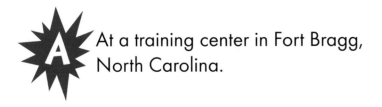

At a training center in Fort Bragg, North Carolina.

Delta teams must think quickly all the time. These soldiers need to surprise the enemy. They learn to blend in with the people around them. No one knows they are operators. They also learn to blend in with the land. They train to work quietly and stay hidden. They learn to use camouflage to sneak up on the enemy.

Soldiers must stay hidden from enemies.

Delta teams are best known for **close combat**. They have excellent fighting skills. Operators practice fighting in small spaces. They can fight without weapons. Or they can make a weapon with things around them. They also practice fighting with weapons. They shoot guns. They launch bombs. They train to kill the enemy.

These men train for close combat.

17

The Home Front

At home, most of the Delta team's time is spent on drills. They practice a mission as if it were real. Some drills are a surprise. Soldiers don't know when the drill is happening. They may not even know if it's a drill or a real mission. An operator is always ready, even for a drill.

Operators use maps to plan their missions.

Delta units study their missions together.

The home front is also where Delta Force returns after a mission. Some missions are successful. Others are not. But all the missions are studied. At home, the team learns about what worked well. They also work out their problems on failed missions.

Delta teams also do security. They are ready if there is an attack. They stay hidden and quiet. You may not even know they are there. But they are. They keep us safe.

Delta Force has also helped the Secret Service. The Secret Service guards the president. Delta Force is there at times too.

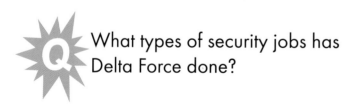

What types of security jobs has Delta Force done?

Delta Force teams help keep the president safe.

Delta Force did security at the Olympic Games in Los Angeles and Atlanta.

Overseas

Delta Force missions are often overseas. They plan carefully. They load their gear on planes. When it is time to go, they slip away. On the mission, snipers wait on top of buildings. Others clear out the enemy. Hostages are rescued. When the job is done, they sneak back home. Quick and quiet. In and out.

A soldier moves quickly on a mission.

Radios help soldiers talk to the rest of their team.

 What other special gear does Delta Force use?

Delta teams use a lot of special gear. They use night vision goggles, or NVGs. Then they can see in the dark. Microphones help them hear the enemy. They can even be far away. Radio gear lets them talk to each other. But it also **encrypts** the signal. Then no one else can understand them.

 They use heat-seeking cameras. These cameras help them find enemies or hostages, even in the dark.

Serving Our Country

Terrorists put our lives in danger. But Delta Force keeps us safe. They stop our enemies. Delta Force missions are often secret. We don't always know what they did to keep us safe. Life in the Delta Force can be deadly. But these soldiers work hard for our safety.

Delta Force soldiers are always ready for a mission.

Glossary

close combat Fighting in small spaces.

encrypt To scramble or mix up information so that no one can understand it without the right code or radio.

fast-roping Using a thick rope to drop from a helicopter quickly.

hostage A person captured and held by the enemy; the enemy keeps a hostage until they get what they want.

operator A member of Delta Force.

terrorist Someone who attacks to cause fear.

unit A group of Delta Force operators.

Read More

Alvarez, Carlos. *Army Delta Force.* Armed Forces. Minneapolis: Bellwether Media, 2010.

Besel, Jennifer M. *The Delta Force.* First Facts. Elite Military Forces. Mankato, Minn.: Capstone Press, 2011.

Riley, Gail Blasser. *Delta Force In Action.* Special Ops. New York: Bearport, 2008.

Websites

American Special Ops: Delta Force
www.americanspecialops.com/delta-force/

How Stuff Works: How Delta Force Works
science.howstuffworks.com/delta-force.htm

Military.com: Delta Force: Missions and History
www.military.com/special-operations/delta-force.html

Index

About the Author

Linda Bozzo is the author of more than 45 books for the school and library market. She would like to thank all of the men and women in the military for their outstanding service to our country. Visit her website at www.lindabozzo.com.